T0354845

Thrive

TOM GEIGER

authorHOUSE®

AuthorHouse™
1663 Liberty Drive
Bloomington, IN 47403
www.authorhouse.com
Phone: 1 (800) 839-8640

Published by AuthorHouse 12/28/2019

ISBN: 978-1-7283-4145-3 (sc)
ISBN: 978-1-7283-4146-0 (hc)
ISBN: 978-1-7283-4147-7 (e)

Complaints are Restraints

What are the issues, who are to blame?
Is it only you that's bothered?
Probably more societal shame!
Let's defeat it not retreat from it.
Show Dignity, have faith in someone more than you,
grow to your Ability.
Don't look in your pockets for day to day Change.
Stand up, Dig In, Speak out, your thoughts, rearranged.
With all on the line, build up your spine
just a moment in time - you can be and who you really are!

Life's Worth

There's a time for fun and a time for words. I'd like to have a word with you. Your beautiful, kind and gentle too, yet this world is opposite through and through. It's difficult as hell to merge the two.

Our time here should not be determined by us, for immediately becoming disastrous. Drunks would stay drunks, thieves remain thieves, depression would rule, what a world we'd have weaved.

A life cut short has no second chances, your vision becomes shattered glances. You go out "as is" at the depths of despair. No soul can be saved for naught has a care. No longer a life to spare.

You arrive to the Lord all broken and torn, a once vibrant spirit now so forlorn. He stares at his gift of precious life given, through eyes of all knowing, sees your exhausted from livin. Yet he wraps his arms around you and loves you as his child, but weeps that your there early because of a world gone wild.

Your new vision of Jesus has moved you instead, choose life and also the treatment you dread.
Hope is the fuel inspiring this move. Immediate death's no longer an option. Satin will cease his obsessive distraction, your decision a wise one, to stay with the Lord, this time observing his loving word.

What we'd like is a new life, that's bearable to live. It comes with conditions, you must be willing to give. Don't be deceived by the treatment received. In this world there is no 100 percent. Most troubles will be dealt with and thus go away, but others may linger and forever stay. The difference will be how you perceive them each day.

Soon finding life in everyday treasures. Unnoticed before due to wayward pleasures. Soon becoming less and less dismayed. For now you are open to what the real world displays, unbelievable as it seems, There are people who really do care!!!!

Rewards of Love

Years multiply with plenty of pain in supply. The object is to turn your head, ignore what you dread, face towards your promised rewards, accept them for a better life, so full of enjoyment, so little strife!

Your promises can be great, even here on earth, once we remove the generational curse.
Know that love comes in all different ways, some not expected, some with delays.

Just knowing your thought of, and in the Lords heart, is the type of reward that I'd soon never part. It might not seem fancy, shiny or new, but know deep down in your soul, GOD gave it to you, Go take a step forward, test the world that you knew. You will see how it's changed, what a wonderful view!

Aging

Age shows us who we really are.
Many fight that, being we've come so far.
Looks go away, getting tired each day.
All this is noticed, yet still brings dismay
The real sadness of age, is the youngness still felt.
Our minds are still feeling the days lived before
With our hearts that still melt about loved ones adored
At a loss to experience all the passion again.
The mistakes we had made, what would we change then

We'd see more, we'd know more, we'd converse daily
For We know how to be better people, holding them near.
There's nothing to prove now, nothing to fear.
Just be who GOD made you, bringing all your love near.
We all tried our best, with the gifts we were given
Regret not, Look not, on the past and keep living

Lovers and Friends

The desire to have another around. We have seen each other, we've already become knowingly attracted, one immediately began to pursue the other at unbeatable odds. Despite numerous failures, They persisted with a positiveness that defies logic as we watched with wondrous intrigue. Neither of us knowing how long our hearts will last, as if the strain and rupture is inevitable. To let this stop us, only to tread water, to lay idle, is not even thinkable. Realize your passion for people and life. Others say much, but we listen little. For passion is our Hope, our Spirit, our reason for being.

The anger in silence

Manifested by not the lack of knowledge, but of the minds' own retention of constant information, and it's ability to reference it, in a moment's notice.

Failure in doing this, can and has created an attitude from others in that you are in fact unknowledgeable. The follow-up on most subjects lacks the contiguous facts, required for debate. Although it is in fact known. It cannot be expressed. Expressed quickly enough to argue.

Do not, however, stop from learning or reading about any subject, or even performing it, due to a loss of proper description. For it is only important that your mind realizes the endless possibilities and potential of your work or passions. Others need to be slowed down to your speed, not theirs!!!

The Early Bird

The start of a day creates passion in some, I look forward to it being done. The course of the day is where I could stay. The mood is all set, your focus met, guiding you forward without breaking a sweat. To go into night with a purpose in mind, that's an achievement rarely to find. To know of a goal and rush up to meet it, gives a person the strength which is always much needed. Early to Rise is great for the Masses, for me I prefer 1000 lashes!!

"Hanging On"

Life's on edge
Bets are hedged
Living with courage
Friends' pledge
In corner wedged

Time has silenced
Emotions restrained

Stay True to Us

A region of land, something as simple as that, can forever change you, a guaranteed fact. You pass through it daily by walking or driving, mingling amongst it's people, some barely surviving.

You say to yourself am I better than them? You question their lot, pretending to know, trying on feelings, "friend or foe". Judging their lives as if having a clue. Not ever stepping a foot in their shoe.

This type of behavior is normal to most and even accepted, surely nothing to boast. We travel our way, they travel theirs, is how many would like it, albeit the stares.

With so many people, so many towns. A tension between us, racism has no bounds. Born out of ignorance, snuff it out as shame. We all need each other, we claim. Let's show all who we are. For we all are the same!

"Your Lot"

How could things be so desperate when everything is fine? You live, you work, your eating, even enjoying a little, at times. The bills are being paid, even on the surface, progress is being made. Your Heart is first to tell you, your meaningless no matter. The gains bring pains, they twist our minds to hopelessness under all its hurtful strain.

You reach out for reality, which agrees with all above, there is no crashing meteor, you need no plastic gloves. You dismiss this as incredulous, as if you could be so wrong. The others don't accept it, but I'll keep my head on strong. My world of course is shrinking, with friendships gone astray, mainly through no contact, some with what I say.

It's sad for only a moment. Then reality strikes again. Your better off without them.

"Not Our World"

Barely a thought through most of our lives, just expecting the same day to day. As much as we know that life's all about change, we choose to ignore it, how personally deranged! Sneaking back in, at an unannounced time, reminding us, we're no match for the Devine. Yes, our minds fool us, that our power on earth, is so overwhelming, we believe it ourselves. Then during our ignorance or unyielding pride, a loved one. an accomplishment, or financial success, is ripped from our grasp leaving us aghast. It burns in your heart, but mostly your mind, you took so much for granted, forgetting to find, the place in between where your loving and kind. We all forget our purpose, try to keep it in mind.

"Searching"

Home
I haven't been home for years
It's an extended tour I'm on
with no end in sight, like a space voyage without the time travel,
The time is going by, creating a sense of urgency to accomplish
something, to complete a task, anything to get home. The day my
home was emptied, the doors locked for the last time, it truly was the
last time. Home has transformed from an actual place with actual
beings, to a feeling. So that is what I'm searching for, a feeling within
me, something that speaks to me and calms me. Something that tells
me I'm home. The past holds the answers for the future. The future
just needs to prove it day by day.

Wherever I am, it's the saddest place. Nothing brings fulfillment or sense of being. This world I've created in my mind, full of distrust, full of anger, full of true despair. So Full that it's empty, senseless, non-productive, and void of Hope. These are the thoughts of a lost man.

"Follow"

Natural wonders aren't all those places we visit, placing stamps in our books, or to view the structures that man or nature has created. No, The natural wonders are us, yes each of us sculpted from a different grain of sand. Growing as families in different regions and lands. If we looked at each other and truly took time to experience, and learn from all cultures, we'd have traveled the world a thousand times over. With all of us together, what a powerful force. Now give us free will, abundant choices, and a reason to judge, we'll separate everytime. Colors won't mix, races divide. Religions are blurred. Which side to decide. My choice is Jesus, to follow his ways. He creates a clear path for all to unite. Let's not disappoint by showing our might, but instead listen to reason knowing he's right.

The Truth
I strain to breathe
Pressure builds in my head
Tears seep from my eyes
My teeth are clenched
My body weary, exhausted
Happiness is gone
Only the Void Remains

"Relax"

Comfort can be reduced to the type of socks you wear to the paper clips you use. The most inane object, sound, or feeling can create comfort.

For myself, it's mostly sounds putting me at ease. A simple rainy evening, a distant train whistle, a favorite song. Plus many others as well. They all calm me to relaxation.

Find Yours and Enjoy

Uncertainties prevalent
Decisions to bide by
Movements robotic
The tasks at hand
Right or wrong
All's set in motion

"Some fight Brave Battles, others defeat themselves!"

"Cowardice is the main ingredient for non-action."

"Thoughts are always the beginning of Actions"

"To start is to Triumph"

"We are only Stronger than, our Problems"

Apologies

How do I manage to set my trap
All the words spoken, being too open.
To late to save fate. Should keep to myself, hesitate

Allowing others their special world
Denying myself my precious word
Watching my interests being unfurled
Dissecting their meaning now sounding absurd

My life, my truths, my loves
Unable to reach my thoughts respect
Looking truth in the eye
Unable to connect

My insides now sick
Why always to lose

"A Man"

What makes a man?
His home, car or style of clothes
The way he thinks or what he knows
His belief in higher powers
The walk he walks, never cowers

Maybe it's work that defines him
Striving to be the best. Or To feel families' love to put him at rest,
no matter the quest, despite the success.

The role he plays in other's lives
Full of concern, with help he arrives.
No reciprocal role is needed for help.
Just having a chance to get one through a day,
without any big miracle, or tales to say.

His burdens are hidden, far from sight.
To alleviate worry about his plight.
He will share all his conquests when the time is right.
You need to believe in him, to advance to new heights.

Your mother's a puzzle

Built piece by piece, each different as the next, one with strength, emotion, and peace. She fits these together all through her life, so completion is never, increasing her strife.

As you grow older you hold on less and less, but those years of exposure, drag you, draw you into the mindlessness. It's a bond that's shared through a lifetime for sure. If you stay strong with your needs it can be endured.

These types of mothers cling on for years. Requiring their children to depend on their love and need to be near. Regardless of your needs. Negating your thoughts, while she needlessly points out all of your faults.

It's selfishness, simple and pure siphoning all energies, leaving no cure. She tries to help, but gets in her way, with constant directives imposed day to day.

They get what they want one way or another, because in this life you have but one Mother!!

"Belief"

Believing is not in the touching, seeing, or hearing, but in the acceptance of what we can't comprehend. The unknown, the certainties or uncertainties that lie before us. Happiness, sorrows, achievements, bereavements, our very own reconcilement. These are what binds us as a people. There is no distinction between us, we all share this profound naivety.

"Moving Forward"

It's our vision for the future
That keeps our lives on course
Not the daily battles
We fight that make it worse
Causing more remorse
We must fight it at its source

This will bring success, for coping day to day,
All that we can hope for is peace and sanity.
The fighting's long and arduous, of course as you'd expect.
Nothing comes so simple once it is a wreck.

Sadness, as in all wars, casualties in wait.
Our minds, our hearts, and wholeness saturated with hate.
There seems no simple passage, neither path nor time to take.
Just look in constant disbelief each new memory you make.

Someday all involved will see the wasted time, but, by then the damage has been done.
No one ever won.
The time was taken by evil.
Enjoyed, consumed and unsalvageable, total upheaval. Unable to recover.
We retreat to heal our wounds.

"Life's Circle"

Generations collide with unruly acts.
Both physically, mentally, and with misplaced facts.
The unknown collision of ages continually exists.
Only far too late with a provisionary list.

The list will elude you if there's no sustained growth.
Making your death more lonely, envisioning both.
We live as we see to live, what comforts us most.
Our beliefs seen through a tunnel, our knowledge to boast.

Realize our being not alone,
We've all broke away from our past and old days.
Each like a rebel, but feeling the power.
Knowing our life, is our life, to live in this hour.

Having been said many times, "like a thief in the night",
Our life goes by quickly, feeling more like a flight.
We flew through the changes, the stresses, our loves.
Now meeting our past, at a level far above.

It's here that we all see life as it truly is.
Possessions so meaningless, our struggles, so small.
The worrisome hours, the workloads so tall.
Intelligence, money, status or fame. We now see as broken, so full of
shame.

Beings not races are particularly clear.

Experiencing this moment is heartfelt sincere.

We are all one in life, just as in spirit.

Making our way to survive with no general guide.

For our end is certain, you will be alone.

If asked of you then if a higher power exists.

Your attitude now would be not to resist.

Only to see into your heart, and feel peace finally persist.

So Close

Touching moments become so vague,
you cannot realize where to wage your next discovery or any rage.
You simply fade away from beauty. Without a cause or useful duty.
All is leading to loneliness, the nauseous feeling of worthlessness.

Even self-esteem eludes us, trying hard not to confuse us.
We try to grasp with all our might, the memories still within our sight.
How long they last is up to us, yet we blame all others, as if just.

The essence of all reality, lies directly at our feet.
Waiting to be picked up to let us dismiss defeat.
To carry on our wayward ways. Our souls inner comfort within a lazy gaze.

In all this twisted wonderment,
The sun shines through as if GOD-sent.
It's glow so soothing, it's warmth felt fast,
calming us to accept our past. As the sun sets, our anxieties pass.
Only hope brings us comfort, comfort at last!!

"To Know"

Why burden each other with your individual expectations.
Why not flow together as if a stream. calming at times,
slowing you both, to floating together under the heat of the sun.
Wishing together for some cool water around your feet.
Now a little faster as to let boulders turn you to waves,
crashing you round into white caps. Much like life itself.

Melding our thoughts as if never diverse,
allowing each to dwell in the other's mind.
Siphoning all knowledge of their being.
Having no idea the same you are, a tangled series,
of sense, sensitivity, insensitivity, and senselessness.
Incoherence at once explained.

There we have come to understand.
To strive for the all knowing of each other.
The quest to relate, to unravel, to take in, and feel the other's all.

Why?

When we find ourselves unoccupied, looking where do we go from
here.
When the roads lead us nowhere, that we haven't been before.
When the activities you loved to do, are so far out of reach.
We have to ask ourselves, why? Why do we stay doing what we do?
Why do we continue dwelling where we care not to be?
What are we working for, certainly not for fun.
Any Reasonable person would be running to get out.
Why, do we stay. Fear…

"The Example"

An empire was built
By a man with a vision
Not haphazardly, unplanned, or by an unlikely decision.

An industry gap or vacuum we say,
Was the catalyst needed to pave the way.
An industrious man, with the skills and foresight,
at this time alone was ready for flight.

The equipment in play required a person of great forethought,
one to verbalize Safety, Quality, and being American Bought.
A product that exuded excellence. Nothing less would suffice.

In a climate so caustic with men getting killed,
the importance of safety was key to fulfill.
His designs, many patented, engineered through and through.
Left nothing to question only to advance and pursue.

The rest is all known, the men's jobs being saved.
Keeping local tradesmen at work. Never having to cave.
Here's a man of great judgement, you can see that for sure,
a man to be remembered, through tests he endured.

Not only out, for his own personal gain.
Helping others as well, during their times of pain.
Not selfish, but giving, showing kindness in ways,

that we'll never know.

To many unfortunates at the lowest of low.

Men like this are so seldom found.

For as tough as he was, he gave his heart by the pound!

Try to remember:

Nothing bad comes from the goodness in your heart.
What can people truly say that can hurt you?
You possess all the strength required to survive!!
All else is nonsense. So Thrive!!!

I love addictive people you can always get them to do more!!!

Everything you do is something DONE!!!!!

Animals

Only the Lord provides the moments, that we are treated to a glimpse.
A rare viewing of his creatures, as they live in the wilderness.
As we occupy unknown areas as a guest.

At times, waiting hours, never seeing a thing.
Then you'll catch a movement of pure beauty, everlasting.
This beauty is ever fleeting yet grips your heart so strong.
For you may never see again, an animal where it belongs.

Roaming the mountains, swimming the seas,
Traversing the deserts, living in trees.
Traveling for miles, flying with ease.
These are the species we wonder upon.
Watching every movement, a spectacle of some great show.

We were long entertained,
before we got in our way.
Now it seems a chore to visit the outdoors.
Waiting again to champion our great gift
Much like before!

Hometown

From the country woods to the city alleyways.
Where the swamps turn to lakes, and the lakes into rivers,
the rivers to oceans. This was our yard, our playground, our ball
courts.
From the inches we knew as young, to the miles as old. As we walked,
then rode bikes, to cars and boats, plus busses and trains, This is
referred to as our backyard,
our neighborhood, our turf, our surf!! No one could tell us about it,
we ruled it. We ridiculed it, we loved it. Then it molded us, defined
us, determined who we would ultimately become, or if we would run.

Over the great expanse of our Vision it would still be, at best, a guess as to our future. Instincts dictate to us that calmness and indifference will not be tolerated. Everyone has a distinct and fervent view of what they and their children will accomplish.

Their reality will be shattered by a never ending onslaught of trials, tribulations and triumphs. Some bought on by themselves, but most have a way of finding you.

What we do know about the future is that if we take our next breath, we are still alive. All else is imagined, engineered, or dreamt up. We will always insist along the way, what our future is, which is how we cope with the unknown.

Disillusioned. at best confusion
Distressed with man's intrusion
This world once heavenly before infusion. Of all things "Man"

Preservation diluted by any actions
Thoughts plus ideas compromised, dismissed as infractions.
More hesitation, less penetration.

Futile the feeling encompassing us
Enduring daily endeavours a must

Ever plausible

A reversal of life, has been set in motion. As you think thoughts you'd never think, not even a notion. The strength of this change is stronger than all. Even if gravity would allow not a fall. This course has been set as far back as birth, cause it's Time that we're fighting to claim our self-worth.

Our thoughts, yes, are changing as well as our looks. The habits we have, the secrets we took. All that's been hiding, will be in plain sight. As our minds deteriorate during this plight. There is no escape, never has been. It's one of life's mysteries amongst another map's pin.

"Widower"

I know he's with you
And that's got to do

Even if I died I'd be by your side

Life here below, is not fun to know
You tire real fast, cause the years fly past

I changed the sheets on the bed, I don't know why.
Thought that I heard that you might stop by,
but I was dreaming, misunderstood your meaning

Know your not coming, but missing you so.
Seeing, Hearing you, seems so but no.

Meeting Spot

There's a happy place
That I know of here, it's the only kind of place, As if you grew up here
Only you and your close friends know where it is. When your all
there, nothing in the world tops this.

Sharing the growing up, you've all been doing. All the big and fancy
plans that have been brewing. Girlfriend. Boyfriend sitting by, hand in
hand, gazing at the stars in the sky. Both feeling closer knowing why.

This place we have, we'll always have. Our feeling good comes out to
play. No one says to put it away. It's welcomed here, and here it will
stay. For beyond this happy place of ours, is an ugly world that waits
to devour.

Worldly Thoughts

Truman, Churchill, Reagan, & Thatcher. There are none of these today. Yes, they overcame many great obstacles, Those situations being over now. As great a people they were, they still fell short in many areas. Much like us as everyday folks, we can only juggle just so many problems, before they overwhelm you. A lot of us believe we give 100% or even 110% (for the most arrogant). The truth is no matter how great a job you think your doing at work or at home, something is always being shorted. It's wonderful to believe the impossible, just know at a certain level it becomes unachievable. I'm not talking giving up dreams here. I'm a dreamer at best.

What I'm saying is World Peace, world Hunger, Poverty, Racism, Justice, Medical, and to be good stewards of our planet, and all living things, to only name a few!! These are all fantastic causes and yes, show some results over time. The point I'm trying to make is that we are not a perfect people. We kill, to provide safety, we destroy to provide luxuries, we hate to feel as if we belong, we do our worse to attain money and power. To go full circle as we all like to say, let's put Money, Power, and Greed at the top of this page and let it bleed through all the problems we have listed. You will see that we all have blood on our hands, simply to survive this world that WE have created, not the world that our Higher Power wanted for us. No higher power for you? Sad, but, No matter we're all here together, that's our only similar bond!!

Love's at the Gate

It's been a while since the smile of love's appeared. It hasn't been a lack of looking. What you see is a pleasure, what's inside is no treasure. That's not meant for me.

It's a struggle to get started, when you think you'll soon be parted. It's that trust creeping in. Lack of confidence is sure to win. To change, is to change the patterns already arranged.

Accomplishments may be many, yet they seldom compare. strengths are your strengths. Shallow is the one with only assets to share. Traveling is another, which grateful for, for sure.

Adapt without adapting is a falsehood to be sure, never getting anywhere, never to endure. The love you seek is genuine, why start the quest whilst towing the line.

Timing

It's not of great consequence that I say No. The word itself is well overdue, through many years and many struggles in real life as well as in my mind, where only Yes endures.

In this world it's a weakness to not argue, to let things go by without issue. Any appearance of not standing up to others' thoughts. As if many of the thoughts are truly worthy to stand up for. A good man will always know when a stand needs to be made.

You Know

There are only a few questions that can be asked which demand your attention. Where am I?, What are my plans?, Is my future to be bright? Will I go peacefully? These questions I guarantee will stop you where you stand. There's not a person alive who hasn't asked themselves. The real question is existence. Why am I here? What purpose do I serve? Am I doing everything I can, to live a full life? Who determines a full life was led? We know these answers, yes we really do. Deep in our hearts, the answer beats ever stronger. We determine our path, no one else is privileged to this. This is one thing we own, however frightful, no matter the fear. Take your steps, the steps you were born with. Take them without consciousness. Live in your world, be at peace with your soul. Know and be who you are!

"Change the cycle"

When the tears appear
There'll be more each year
The longer you live
The more of you, you give

All things in time grow weary
Dreams are no different
Thoughts of wonder fade
The world's crept in to invade

When everyday looked promising
It's darker now, more menacing
You turn your head, not to see
Your dreams being crushed by reality

Reality is relevant
never a hand be lent
accomplish your tasks
In your rewards you'll bask

See your dreams through
Don't allow any be mislead
For you deserve not to be blue
After all it was you who had bled

Other Side

The scene in the glass changes as you pass, meaningless at first so difficult to grasp.

A shape distorted, glare of light diverted. Figures appear, desperate to be visually clear.

Your mind clicks, an eye picks, seeing quick. Who are they, so familiar, right in front of me. Many loved ones had passed, being free. Could it be?

"The Space"

Is it necessary to fill a void?
You know,that vacancy that
everyday makes you feel annoyed.
Can being busy all the time
make life all that much more sublime

If a comfort capsule were to exist
would it contain only you with your busy list?
The possibilities of this are real.
Go find another, let that past one heal.
Enjoy your life create surreal

"Blind Success"

As a young man he used lessons he learned to aggressively handle his opponents for the respect he earned.

As he ventured into the world, there was a reoccurring theme, his mind handled all, struggling it seemed. He was quick to respond and worked towards goals to achieve, a much better life Then he had ever received.

It was a tough life he chose, with long hours away. Virtually alone, though who'd ever say. If truth be told there'd be hell to pay. Hell paid many a visit in life and in work.creeping into all aspects to reap havoc of sorts.

Trying to pick up the pieces with his life torn apart, slowly filling the void of a ripped open heart. This never stop attitude continued for sure, but lying in the midst of all accomplished.

There were no doubts now about his survival, being against it all, there was no rival.

"Decision"

Try to speed but find your slowing
Feel the breeze the wind is blowing
Act as if it's easy rowing
It's not a lie, it's the fact of knowing.

Paths taken from this point matter
Not a simple painting splatter
Choices, decisions, must be made
Not in haste, not in water's wade

Thoughts required, past inspired
Life lived not cheapened, dreams desired
Decisions using all mind's strength
A willingness to take to what length

Answers swirl in the air around
A knowing it was time, so profound
Can a heart be truly trusted?
Or a mind simply adjusted?

So come with an answer, come with a parade
Cause nothing in life beats a charade.
Let them all wonder!!

We've been lead to believe of our greatness within, how everyone touches someone's life for some reason, at the time befitting their need.

"Evil"

Evil, Depression's greatest friend
Welcomes all discontents a hand to lend. First by confirming all your
worst fears, then questioning your every move, sweeping your mind
clear of all rational thought.

"Over Stim"

Our reliance on constant entertainment, to end all boredom or appearance of such. Takes us away from thoughtful processing of our view of the world. It creates non articulation of the facts. People using "feelings" as a judgement.

"Friends"

"In all the world, there are few closer to tell your dreams or thoughts to than friends."

Most friendships when young seem based on fear. Fitting in, someone to bond with, keep near. Talking of family, classes at school, and the fun things you do, that make you feel cool.

A little older, you share your thoughts. Visions of grandeur, aspirations sought. Discussing world wonders attainable to each, but which ones to chase. They're all within reach.

With school mostly behind you, the wildness ceased. Your focused again on which wheels to grease!
Friends are dividing, going their ways, talking of meeting on some distant days.

Some you rely on to get through your days, others are beside you in various ways. As your close ones get married you enjoy life at hand. Building careers, chasing dreams, creating your brand.

As time dwindles them down, a thought enters your head. Which can I count on which one of my friends? They're all now so different, some live far away. The closer ones influence you in uncertain ways.

As far as your friends, you can count on one hand! The folks to rely on you'll hardly understand.

In all the world, there are few close To tell your dreams or thoughts to than friends.

"Go when he calls"

Life in a balance
Yet unknown to many
Thoughts that are challenged
Within your own mind
Answers not known or able to find

Don't whisper the word or action to take.
The most desperate of all things in our world of fate.
It's crucial to focus on the gifts.
The beauty, the wonders, whose loving spirit lifts.

This is a time when all crushes your heart.
All the beliefs in your mind disappear.
As you look out for answers, know there is one, the same one, who already knows your fears.

You can leap from this life, never healing your spirit, so easy a way to choose. Or stay here and search for a healing, a healing that your whole self soothes.

We don't know why we all are different. What we do know is that there's strength in us all. That right there's all we need, to get us through. So the Lord alone can come save you.

"Brevity"

Brevity is a concept lost to me
It has cost me much in my personal and professional world.
A type of secrecy really, not telling it all
Always thought a form of lying.
If telling a story, tell it all!
If parts are left out, Which ones?
They might have been just the descriptive words needed.
Truthfully very little needs to be said, the portions left out create
A mysterious tone, and regardless the story is told
So Brevity is a form of Bold!!!

Printed in the United States
By Bookmasters

Printed in the United States
By Bookmasters